# Who Is the "I Am"?

## Psalm 46:10

## Knowing Your Worth to God

Deanna Dotson

ISBN 979-8-89428-094-3 (paperback)
ISBN 979-8-89428-095-0 (digital)



Christian Faith Publishing
832 Park Avenue
Meadville, PA 16335
www.christianfaithpublishing.com

Printed in the United States of America

To my Mom and Daddy.

# Contents

# *Introduction*

Written by my husband, David Dotson

Who are you? Have you ever asked yourself that question? Have you ever been told that you are a mistake or that you will never amount to anything in life? Have you ever been told that you are ugly or that you are a bad person?

Now let me ask you a question. Does God make mistakes? Let's take a look at what God's word says.

> For everything God created is good, and nothing is to be rejected if it is received with thanksgiving. (1 Timothy 4:4)

> Though he falls, he shall not be utterly cast down: For the Lord upholds him with His hand. (Psalm 37:24)

We learn from these two verses that God does not make mistakes, and if we love and fully trust God and follow His will for us no matter our tribulations, everything will work out for the glory of God.

The Bible tells us in Psalm 139:13, "For You formed my inward parts; You covered me in my mother's womb." God created us and knitted us together in our mother's womb. He personally handcrafted each and every one of us. So if God does not make mistakes and He made you, *you* are not a mistake.

The following writings that you are about to read come from the heart of a very special and courageous woman. She is a woman who has an agape love for all people. No matter your background, no matter your past, she loves you. She loves you enough to share her testimony and her love for God.

Friends, I am honored to call this woman my wife and soulmate, my heavenly blessing here on earth, Mrs. DeAnna Dotson.

# Who Are You? Who Does God Say You Are?

Second Corinthians 5:17 says, "Therefore if any man be in Christ, he is a new creature: old things are passed away; behold, all things are become new." God makes no mistake with His creation. In His eyes, you are beautiful. You are not ugly; you are not a mistake. God doesn't make mistakes.

Yes, mistakes were made in the past, and possibly someone even hurt you in such a way that you thought you couldn't move on. One of the weapons that the enemy likes to try and use against us is bringing up our past. Perhaps you were called harsh names by someone you thought loved you or who was a dear friend. You have held on to those memories of those horrible names and subconsciously you have defined yourself by those words.

This is what I want you to do: Write down those words on an imaginary piece of paper. Now, imagine yourself crumbling up that piece of paper in your hands and throwing it away (over your shoulder and behind your back). Now here's the hard part. *Don't* pick up that piece of paper; *give* it to Jesus!

You're not worthless; you are someone who Jesus loves very much. He knows what you have been through and is saddened from it. He takes all our pain away, all the guilt and shame we carry around. The struggles from everyday life, He's there too. Let Jesus fight our battles for us.

Jeremiah 29:11 says, "For I know the thoughts that I think toward you, saith the Lord thoughts of peace, and not of evil, to give you an expected end."

What's in the past is in the past. You may have been an addict, but that doesn't reflect who you are now. Don't let your past determine your now and your future. No one should bring up your past again. In *Psalm 103:12*, we are told, "As far as the east is from the west, so far hath he removed our transgressions from us." When we repent of our sins, God does not remember them. When God forgives, He doesn't bring them back up to us ever again. The enemy (Satan) just wants you to relive it and not be happy. Time and time again, he's showed his ugly head bringing up my past, trying to make me feel bad all over again.

However, the enemy (Satan) will try to take you back to your past, but your past has been forgiven. Yesterday is gone, and today is a new beginning. Just as Christ has forgiven us, we also should forgive ourselves. You are here for a reason, and God has a purpose for you and your future.

Everyone messes up, but you know what? It's okay. God loves you no matter what. You're not that person anymore, and you don't have to stay in that cold, dark, and lonesome place anymore. You are a new creation in Him bought with a price. God's love and mercy is never-ending, and you're not who you were no matter your circumstances, no matter what you have done.

God doesn't hold that against you. All you have to do is ask for forgiveness and repent of your wrongdoings and your sins. God is just and faithful to forgive. First John 1:9 says, "If we confess our sins, He is faithful and just to forgive our sins, and to cleanse us from all unrighteousness." He's always going to be there for you no matter what. He'll never leave you nor forsake you. God is gracious, loving. He is compassionate, caring, forgiving, and selflessness. His forgiveness is more than words can express. Most importantly, His love for you will never change, and that's why His perfect sacrifice was His only Son.

Just think, you are so important to God that He sent His only son to die for you and me. He didn't have to, but He loves us so much that Jesus laid down His life willingly for us. John 3:16 says, "For God so loved the world, that He gave His only begotten Son, that whosoever believeth in Him should not perish, but have ever

We try to fill that special place with worldly things: sex, drinking, drugs, money, selfishness, etc. However, after trying to fill that special place with worldly things, you realize that only God can fill that special place in your heart.

If God can turn a bad situation around for me, bringing me out of the pits of hell, He can do the same for you. With God, all things are possible, and He can take something broken and make it whole again. That goes for you too if you allow God to work in your life. He can do a mighty work in you. He doesn't make you go alone in anything. He holds you up even when you think it's impossible to go on. He holds the sparrow in flight; He doesn't let her fall.

# 1

## Deanna's Personal Testimony

Nestled in a Northeast Tennessee valley surrounded by the Cherokee National Forest, Erwin, Tennessee, is surrounded by mountains in all directions. To the north, you have the Buffalo Mountain; to the west, the Rich Mountain; and to the south and east, you have the beautiful Unaka Mountains. The world-famous Appalachian Trail and beautiful Nolichucky River are just east of Erwin.

Yes, Erwin, Tennessee, is a beautiful and picturesque place. However, Erwin has somewhat of a dark history too.

In 1916, Erwin became known for carrying out the only known public execution of an elephant on September 13, 1916. The event that led up to this public execution involved a five-ton Asian elephant named Mary occurred on September 11, 1916, in Kingsport, Tennessee. Mary performed in the Sparks World Famous Shows Circus for many years, and she was known for playing musical instruments and throwing baseballs.

Mary's keeper was a homeless man named Red Eldridge. Even though he was not qualified to work as an elephant keeper, he was hired by the Sparks World Famous Shows Circus. Mr. Eldridge had only been Mary's keeper for two days when the incident occurred.

During a parade through Kingsport, Tennessee, it was reported that Mr. Eldridge while riding on Mary's back, prodded her behind one of her ears with a hook after she had reached down to eat a piece of watermelon lying on the ground. Obviously, this enraged Mary, and she threw Mr. Eldridge onto the ground and stepped on him.

Mary was detained and placed on a railcar and transported to Erwin, Tennessee. It was here, in the Clinchfield Railroad yard, that she was hanged by the neck from a railcar-mounted industrial derrick in the presence of over 2,500 people. After her execution, she was buried next to the tracks in the railyard.

The town of Erwin remembers Mary during a yearly festival and elephant art auction. Local artists display their works of art of painted small elephant sculptures; and then, the art pieces are auctioned off and all proceeds go to The Elephant Sanctuary in Hohenwald, Tennessee.

Another black eye for Erwin occurred in 1918, when a group of white citizens was involved in the murder of a black man. After the murder of this man, all other black citizens from Erwin were forced out of town by a white mob. Erwin had officially become a "Sundown Town." The term "Sundown Town" came from signs that were posted throughout the town that read, "Colored People had to leave town by sundown."

By March of 1983, all the "Sundown Town" signs were gone and the talk of "Murderous Mary" the elephant was just spoken of on occasion. What I remember as a little girl, living in this small northeast Tennessee town, are not memories of racism but memories of playing outside, running around barefooted and feeling the cool grass under my feet, swinging on my favorite tire swing on warm sunny days, and playing with my older sister, Alisha, who I loved to torment.

My daddy and mom faithfully took me to church on a regular basis; I don't ever recall missing a service. Singing the old hymns, and I do mean the *old…slow…*hymns and getting into God's word was so important to my family and me.

When I was about five years old, my daddy had a heart attack, and he had to have open heart surgery in which the doctors did a five-vessel bypass on him. Daddy was really sick for quite some time. After his long road of recovery, Daddy and Mom both took a job as "house parents" at a children's home in Greeneville, Tennessee.

Daddy and Mom packed up all our belongings, and with Alisha and me in tow, we moved to Greeneville.

Our new life at the children's home was so much fun. There were so many children there, and I made a few new friends. On the children's home campus, there was a gym where we could play and an indoor swimming pool where I learned to swim. But the coolest thing out of all the things that were there were the horses that we could ride. I mean, come on, who doesn't like riding horses. Right?

Our home was located right next to the school, so my sister and I walked to school. Some of my teachers were very nice, and some were not so nice. Oh well, I survived it, and just like any elementary school aged student…the struggle was real.

During my second-grade year, we ended up having to move and leave the children's home where my daddy and mom worked. This was one of the first times in my life that I felt a sense of confusion because we had no place to go; I felt like a feather being blown around in a thunderstorm.

We found ourselves staying with some of our friends, and they graciously allowed us to stay until we were able to find a place to rent. My daddy found work as a custodian and grounds keeper at the local high school. My daddy was a hard worker, and he did what he had to do—even though his health continued to deteriorate on a daily basis.

It was a stroke that caused my daddy to become permanently disabled. However, even after his stroke, he worked on a farm in exchange for our monthly rent. My daddy was not a quitter. My daddy never gave up on his family. My daddy loved mowing hay, out on the tractor, working with cattle and building fences. If it had to do with outdoors, my daddy loved doing it. No matter what my daddy was doing out in the field, I wanted to be right there with him. Yes, I was a "daddy's girl." Wherever my daddy went, I was there also, Daddy's little shadow.

My daddy taught me how to drive a tractor, move cattle from one field to another, and build barbed-wire fence. I remember my daddy and I building over five miles of fence together. During one of our "fence building" adventures, I remember I was driving a fence post down into the ground and I came up a little too high with the post driver. Next thing you knew, the post driver flipped back and hit me in the head. Hearing a loud *dong* noise echoing through my head, I could hear my daddy laughing and saying, "*Dong…dong.*" I will not lie, it did hurt a little, but it was kind of funny.

One day, my daddy put me on the forks of the tractor and lifted me up into the air while driving through the fields. My mom would have flipped out if she would've have seen that, but I absolutely loved it. I did not fear anything; I was with my daddy, my hero.

My mom soon found out that she was pregnant with my brother. Eli was born in 1992, and I was nine years old, and my sister was thirteen. Eli and I were really close growing up; Alisha and I, not so close.

When I was thirteen years old, my family and I moved back to Erwin. Daddy's health continued to deteriorate, but that did not stop him. My daddy loved being outside and fishing. He was a true man of God. He and Mom always made sure that my siblings and I knew about God. My daddy and Mom loved us very much, and they made sure that God was in our home and in our lives.

Daddy was stern when he needed to be, but gentle as a lamb at other times. I sure received my fair share of whoopin's; I deserved a lot more than what I was given.

I have always had a problem with my mouth getting me in trouble. If arguing with my mom was a sport, I would be a champion. I am talking big golden trophies and biggest first-place, blue-ribbon kind of champion. Need I say more?

I always had to have the last word, and that got me in trouble quite a bit. One day, my mom and I were conversating—yeah right, we'll call it conversating. Well, anyway, in good ole Deanna fashion, I was running my mouth and arguing with my mom while we were riding in the car with daddy. Daddy told me to hush, but I wouldn't do it. For some reason, I just had to keep running my mouth.

The next thing I remember is my daddy pulling the car over to next to the local pharmacy and the car coming to a complete stop. In one swift move, Daddy got out of the car while at the same time pulling me out too. Next thing you know, he had already had a switch in his hand…how he got a switch in his hand so fast, I never know. I definitely deserved that whooping for all my stubbornness.

For some reason, my mouth always got me grounded and a well-deserved whooping. One would think to be quiet after so much, but no, not me.

Growing up with my two siblings, Alisha and Eli, you could always find us outside, jumping on the trampoline, swinging free as a bird on the tire swing, shooting hoops, or splashing in the ice-cold creek that flowed behind our house. My brother Eli became familiar with that cold water; I would often baptize him every chance that I got. I'm sure he didn't like that too much, but we played anyway.

I remember how we would make mudpies, or that's what we called them. Most likely, they were cow patty pies; needless to say, none of us had the guts to taste them.

When Eli was younger, he suffered from seizures and asthma, so we played indoors a lot. We would make these amazing blankets covered forts. At times, Eli was hospitalized due to his seizures and asthma, but praise God, he grew out of them, and he is healed to this day.

Growing up with my older, meaner sister, Alisha, she would always pick on me. So what do little sisters do best? Get revenge…

I remember one day, in the dead of winter, she and I were carrying firewood into our house. Needless to say, I saw a large piece of ice lying on the ground. So I thought to myself, as Alisha was bent over picking up firewood, *I will just chunk it at her.* She rose up just at the right time. So mind you that I have no aim. I meant to hit her on the shoulder with that large piece of ice, but it ended up hitting her right square between her eyes. I just knew I was going to get into trouble, but to my surprise, I didn't. This little sister always had something up her sleeve.

However, she didn't learn her lesson. She would still nag and pick on me; I guess she forgot about the ice incident. Needless to say, we had our times we really didn't get along. One day, I had a wooden ruler in my hand, and I thought to myself, *I wonder how she would feel if I just smacked her in the face?* Well, let me tell you, she found out how it felt. Not long after, my daddy heard about the ruler incident, I got a well-deserved whipping. Needless to say, that didn't stop me from finding ways to pay my sister back for picking on poor, innocent me.

One day, we were out playing in the deep snow. We decided to use Daddy's sled, and we had no idea how to go sledding. So Alisha and I decided to lay down on our bellies to ride the sled. I was on the bottom and Alisha sat on top of me. We started going down the snow-covered hill really fast, and the next thing I knew, Alisha fell off and caused the sled to make a turn-on-a-dime turn. Needless to say, I was launched off that sled like a rocket, and the sled spun around and hit me in the face. I had a nice shiner to show off for several days.

As the years went by and we grew older, Alisha and I loved to play fight. Swapping licks with one another and pinning each other down on the trampoline; again, I don't have a very good aim. I gave her two nice shiners: one to match the other.

In 1999, I was sixteen years old, and we moved to Elizabethton, Tennessee. We were happy to move there because we were closer to our church. Mom was working at the local Walmart, and my daddy was on disability retirement due to his health issues.

My daddy might have had health issues, but he loved going fishing and quilting. Every chance he got, he would be headed down to Watauga Lake to fish for trout, catfish, and bass. He loved having fish fries for the church. Fishing was definitely his favorite past time.

He always enjoyed making people smile, and he loved quilting. Not only did my daddy enjoy sewing and quilting and making us beautiful quilts. More importantly, he sewed threads of love for our family. These threads are threads that will never tear, fray, or break.

My momma always enjoyed baking foods, cakes, pies, and candies and giving them away for people to enjoy. Soon after moving to Elizabethton, I was seventeen years old, and I started working at the local Long John Silvers. I worked there throughout high school, and I met my first husband, Richard, during this time. I was young, crazy, and what I thought to be "madly in love."

The time came when he mumbled the words with a blank expression on his face, "Will you marry me?" At first, I didn't take him seriously, so I nonchalantly answered, "Sure." Well, he was serious…

We considered just eloping, but that really broke my parents' hearts. I remember my little daddy sitting on his porch rocking chair just crying. My daddy's face was reflecting the pain of a broken heart.

Instead of eloping, we planned a full wedding within a month, and we married on November 30, 2001. Richard was nineteen and I was eighteen, and we both had no idea what we were doing.

After getting married, I grew up really quick. Learning to pay bills, having responsibilities that I never had before, this marriage thang wasn't what it was cracked up to be. It was definitely not what the Hallmark channel made it out to be. All that ooshey, gooshey stuff, yeah, that never happened; love definitely does not pay the bills. We thought we were madly in love before we married; needless to say, it all changed after the "I dos."

By age twenty, I had started a new job at the Walmart, working in the shoe department. I had been working there approximately a few months, and I was moved upfront and promoted as a cashier. As the months went by, I found out I was pregnant, and boy the morning sickness really wasn't like what the Hallmark channel said it would be. As my pregnancy progressed, I absolutely loved feeling my baby move and kick; it was the best thang ever. I didn't know what I was in for, awaiting the birth of our baby. I've had been around babies all my life, but I didn't know the first thang about becoming a mommy.

We found out that we were having a girl, and then on January 18, 2005, Anna arrived. She weighed in at 6 lbs., 2 oz., and she was 18 inches long. She was the tiniest little baby, and she looked so fragile. She had swallowed the amniotic fluid, which caused her to stop breathing on us twice. She spent the first four days of her life in an incubator with all these tubes and oxygen. This momma's heart sank as I watched her lying there helplessly, fighting for her life. After God's healing touch, we were finally able to bring her home after the long four days of heartache, thinking she wasn't going to make it.

Growing up as a child, Anna loved being adventurous, always running around like she was flying. She would be smiling from ear to ear, playing with her strawberry shortcake blanket and Care Bears. Now she's eighteen and the strong silent type. I don't see her with that big smile these days, she mostly keeps to herself. Texting, talking with her friends, drawing her plague doctor characters is what she likes best. On occasion, she dresses as a plague doctor with her friends. As I have watched her grow up over the years, she's become a very beautiful young woman.

The years went by, and our marriage was really rocky; most times we wouldn't get along. Anna was three by this time, so I thought just maybe having another baby would fix our marital problems. Well, I decided to go off birth control, without telling my husband what I had planned. Of course, and not long after, I found out I was pregnant. At first, I was really hesitant to tell my husband the news that we were going to have another baby. I decided to lie and say I had missed a dose or two, but in reality, that was farthest from the truth. Nine months later, our second baby was born. A little boy who we named Andrew; he weighed 5 lbs., 10 oz., and he was 18 inches long.

Needless to say, I wouldn't take anything for either of my children, but staying and getting pregnant didn't fix our problems. We fought even more. There were times I left out the door to just to get away.

Andrew grew over the years, and he's really rambunctious. At times, he is very loud; stomping throughout the house (sir stomps a lot) is a sport to him. He loves slamming doors (it's music to his ears).

He's not had an easy life; he's been bullied most his life. He's quite the social butterfly, and he's never met a stranger. He loves playing games and running around like he's in the military shooting toy guns at things. He's always bringing me his halo figures and Transformers and telling me their complete history.

Andrew's fifteen now and getting ready to go to high school. He's been diagnosed with ADHA, OCD, and Tourette's syndrome, and that's why he's been treated different all his life. Many are too quick to judge a book by its cover instead of giving someone a chance. Even some of our family, and sadly some church family, won't give him a chance. It truly breaks this momma's heart seeing the mistreatment that he has endured. His love for God is amazing, and I believe his prayers really touch heaven.

After eleven years of marriage, I was finally done. Satan had started getting in my head and heart, I started seeing guys outside of our marriage. Every chance I had I stayed away from the house, either going to my parents' house or going to see guys. One day while working at Walmart, this guy walks in and puts his charm on thick.

I fell right into Satan's trap, right where he wanted me. I started having a relationship with this Mr. Charm. Satan had his grip on my soul and heart, pulling me more toward a world of sinfulness. You think life is better on the other side of the fence, or possibly the grass greener, but I went from the frying pan and straight into the fire. I had no idea what I was getting myself into. He was charming and said all the right words in the beginning.

I had never been a cheater, but I had become one. At this time, my husband had no idea as to what I was up to. It came time for our eleventh-year anniversary, and it was time to tell him. Needless to say, he didn't take the news very well. I had my mind made up. I was blinded by lust, and I had someone showing me attention.

A few weeks went by, and I became really mean to my husband, rubbing certain things in his face. Mr. Charm and I would take pictures together and send them to him, just to be mean. When Satan has his blinders on you, you don't see anything else around you. It didn't matter who got hurt along the way, I was on top of the world—wrong. I had fallen into the claws of Satan and his lies, and Mr. Charm was the bait to get me to leave my husband.

I was playing a dirty game, which at the time I thought was funny. I knew better than that because I was raised to be respectful to others. Unfortunately, I had become downright spiteful.

Once again, I was planning on leaving my husband for (Mr. Charm). Little did I know what was about to happen and how my world would be turned upside down. It was like a bull in a china shop, and all chaos was about to come crashing down on me. In all my selfishness, I had no cares in the world about hurting my family, most importantly my Father in heaven.

Then early one December morning, without any warning, it struck like a tornado. My doorbell rang, and I thought there must be something wrong with one of my family members. I opened my front door, and to my surprise, there stood a man in a ski mask holding a gun in his hand. It was still dark, and the sun had not started to rise yet, but I could tell this person was a man because of his voice and his silhouette.

When I heard his voice, even though he was trying to disguise it, I had a good idea who it was. As the cold wind blew in my face, he grabbed me, and I felt the barrel of the gun being forced against my forehead.

I remember the fear that overcame me; not just for me, but more importantly for my children who were sleeping in their bedrooms. I immediately told the man that I had no money, but I had a feeling he wasn't there to rob me of money. As he stood there pressing the barrel of the gun against my forehead, he asked me a question that affirmed my suspicion about who this man was. He asked me if I knew the guy who I was cheating with. I answered, "Yes."

He forced me to put a hoodie on backward so as to obscure my vision, and he then tied my hands behind my back. He forced me out of my house and placed the gun to the back of my head and guided me to his car. He placed me in the front passenger seat, and he drove the car down the road to a nearby church parking lot.

I knew exactly where we were because I could just barely see through the hoodie I was wearing. My abductor then ordered me to call Mr. Charm and tell him, "Come down to the parking lot where we were at because he was going to kill him." I told my abductor that Mr. Charm was at work and then he told me, "You're going to give me what I want." I said to him, "Please don't," and he answered me with a stern "Shut up."

I'm going spare the details because my children may read this one day, but I will tell you that he forced me to the back seat, and he raped me. When he was finished with me, he redressed me and placed me back in the front seat. He told me, "The best thing to do is to stay with your husband, and this never happened." He drove me to the street that my house was on and forced me out of the car.

Standing behind me, he untied my hands, took my hoodie off, and told me, "Start walking, and if you turn around, I'll kill you."

Looking back, I wished I had kicked him in the face and broke his jaw, but at the end of the day, "Vengeance is mine," saith the Lord. When I arrived back to my home, my front door was locked, and I had no way of getting back inside. I remember sitting down on the porch steps with the feeling numbness consuming my entire body and mind. No, I didn't run to the neighbor's house to call for help; I just wanted the situation to just go away. Not long after, my husband returned home from work and saw me sitting on the front porch.

He was confused as to why I was sitting on the porch, locked out of the house. I finally told him what had happened, and he took me to the hospital to receive treatment. Being treated in the emergency room was so humiliating. I was in emotional overload as I went through the rape examination.

As they took DNA and hair samples from my body, I thought that the examination would never end. The questions that they were required to ask me were so embarrassing. I literally felt sick, dirty, and humiliated. I felt like I was in a nightmare, and I just wanted to wake up. All I wanted to do was forget about it and move on with my life.

Living in fear of this might happen again made me sick to think about. I had to live for my children and put this far behind me. Life wasn't going to be that simple for the next eleven months; my husband, Richard, and I divorced, and my statement that I had given to the police was being questioned over and over again. I had lost all hope in humanity.

Finally, the DNA results came back and my abductor and rapist was my ex-husband's father. Finally, the answers I was needing, and had waited for, put an end to all the vigorous questioning and negative speculations from the county police officers. They were finally on my side, instead of accusing me of making the whole thing up.

During that year, I had moved in with Mr. Charm. His charming personality ended after I moved in; and he became verbally, mentally, physically, and sexually abusive. The abuse was agonizing, and it was repeated over and over on a daily basis.

It didn't just happen in the bedroom but continued throughout our whole house. His cursing threats toward me sent me into a state of depression and broke my soul. I would go into work really down, but I would put on a front for my coworkers, trying not to show that something was wrong. In reality, life was very hard, and my friends at work could see it all over my face. I would say I was fine, but truth be told, I was lying. I started losing quite a bit of weight and looking really unhealthy: getting down to eighty-six pounds.

Not only was my body in an unhealthy state, but I also started drinking alcohol and smoking marijuana. I looked like death warmed over: very skinny, with depressive thoughts of thinking I wasn't pretty enough. I felt I was worthless and had no value to anyone, and I had no family or friends to turn to. I felt all alone in this world. My family had turned their backs on me, and I had no place to go. I stayed in this relationship thinking that's all I had in this life. I felt that no one would want a woman who had baggage—two children and who had cheated on her husband.

I was broken down to nothing, why would anyone want this woman? I had become the prodigal daughter that no one wanted to deal with. I was an embarrassment to my whole family, except my dearest Aunt Violet. She stood by me no matter what, no matter the wrong I was doing, and the sin I was living in; she never once judged nor condemned me. Even though the abuse was so severe, it was a place to stay without being out on the streets with two children.

One day, while Anna and Andrew were at their dad's house, I finally had taken all that I could. After all the accusations of cheating, all the physical abuse, especially the mental abuse and sexual abuse, I was done. I finally was able to get up the courage and leave him. I was going home, and I didn't know what to expect. I didn't know whether my family would even have me or not.

I called my brother Eli and asked if I could stay a night with him and his wife, Katie. They welcomed me home, and they didn't ask any questions. The next morning, I showed up at church not knowing what Mom and Daddy would say. My daddy and I locked eyes with each other, and we both just cried. As we embraced one another, I will always remember what my daddy had whispered in my ear, "You've not been shunned."

Mom and I had quite a bit of issues to work out as she was holding onto all the hurt I had put her through. Rightfully so, I couldn't blame her. Needless to say, it definitely didn't happen overnight, and it took a bit for us to have forgiveness with one another. My mom and I are both stubborn and set in own ways. Neither one of us wanted to admit we were wrong. It finally came down to me swallowing my pride and apologizing.

After being home for a while, my children and I got an apartment, and I started working at a local restaurant, the Texas Road House. I was getting my life put back together, getting back in church and raising two children on my own. Unfortunately, I started slipping back into my old ways. I was living an unholy lifestyle and started sleeping with other guys just to feel alive. Needless to say, that didn't fill the void that I so desperately needed in my life.

Satan really had his blinders on me, and I was drifting further away from God. Father God allowed me to hit rock bottom before I was awakened to my sinful lifestyle. I went through several guys thinking that maybe this is the one who would be the right guy for me…nope, think again.

I wasn't content being alone and single. I just wanted someone to notice me, and maybe ask me out. Not to get me into bed but just to be a gentleman and kind to me. You know, someone who would treat me like a lady, someone who would truly love me. I was looking in all the wrong places, but God had other plans. He kept shutting the doors to possible relationships, I never understood as to why. God knew better than I He had one for me I just had to be patient. I'm so glad God opened my eyes and showed me my worth in Him.

He took this dirty, tainted woman, who had done so much bad and washed me white as snow. I was carrying around shame and guilt that I no longer had to carry. I realized that I am a child of God who had been made clean. I'm no longer a slave to sin. I am redeemed, restored, and forgiven. I'm a daughter of the most-high God. Forgiveness and restoration were beginning.

There were so many times my past kept creeping back up and showing its ugly head. I didn't think I was forgivable. You know what, though, through all my mishaps, failures, and running from God, He was there the whole time, extending His hand toward me, waiting for me to take hold. I was running through life, doing my own thing for a while. Yes, I went to church here and there, but I wasn't living for God. I was just going through the motions.

During the chaos of being a single mom and raising my two children on my own, my little daddy got sick. We eventually had to put him in a nursing home for twenty-four-hour care that my family could not adequately provide for him. We all had families, jobs, and responsibilities that would keep us from providing the care that he needed.

Every chance I had I went to see him; his smile would light up the room. No matter how he felt, he always smiled. He would make funny faces, looking like Popeye, with one eye closed and sticking out his tongue underneath his false teeth. He made us all laugh no matter the circumstances. My mom really did what she could to make sure he had the help he needed. Placing him in a nursing home was one of the hardest decisions that we had to make as a family.

After my daddy's courageous battle with dementia and heart failure, my little daddy went to his heavenly home. We all were grieved over the loss of him, but God gave us a special gift, the gift of memories. We know that the day will come that we will meet him in the air and see our Savior, face-to-face.

I've had all kinds of struggles along the way; missing my Daddy barely making it, being a single mom wasn't easy. My faith in God didn't leave me, and He's the one who brought me through the storms of my life. If it weren't for Him, I wouldn't be here today. I'm not where I want to be, but I'm not where I was. God has transformed me into a better woman than I was. I was an adulterous, selfish woman, sleeping around and I only thought about myself. The mother I was doesn't exist anymore; that woman is gone. Thanks to God and my praying parents, that's the reason I'm here today. I gave my heart to Christ in 2018, and since that time, I have fallen and made mistakes. God has picked me back up over and over. I have learned that I do have a purpose in God. I have given Him my everything: my life, my home, and my children. It was the best decision of my life, giving my whole life to Christ. I had a long road ahead of me, and I let God take the reins of my life. I was letting go and letting God take over, instead of Deanna doing what she wanted to do.

I'm so thankful to my Lord and Savior and how far He has brought me. My life has changed so much for the better, and my children and I started going back to church on a regular basis. During one of our worship services, I was asked to join the dance team; that's where I found my purpose and calling.

There were times I would go the wrong way or bump someone, but they were gracious with me. Now I'm dancing every chance I get with my fellow brothers and sisters of Messiah. In 2021, I had our house prayed over and anointed, giving all that I had to God. As we were praying God showed one of our pastor's wife a vision. God showed her that I was a new creation in Him, being brand-new and cleansed like a new virgin and lying next to my bridegroom (Yeshua) Jesus. In that moment, I cried like a baby; I really didn't think I was worthy. How could God want me after all I had done to Him? He cleansed and changed me in that instance, and I couldn't wait to tell everyone what had happened.

A few months went by, and our pastor started preaching a series of sermons about forgiveness. It was during these sermons that I started feeling a tug at my heart. During one of our Friday night worship services, our pastor stated that the Holy Spirit had given him a word. He said the Holy Spirit was saying that someone needed to be set free from their past sins and hurts. Immediately, I dropped to my knees and started sobbing uncontrollably. It was like the Holy Spirit had pierced my soul and was speaking to me.

I had carried so much guilt and shame around for far too long. As I stood back up, my sisters in Yeshua surrounded me, laying hands on me they started fervently praying. It was at that moment I was able to let go and forgive each and every man, guy, and boy who had hurt me throughout my life. No, they had no clue that I had chosen to forgive them, and that's okay, but God knows, and that my brothers and sisters is what matters the most. I chose to forgive; if I don't, how can God forgive me? You see, it starts with you asking for forgiveness, then you can forgive others. We can't hold onto grudges and hatred that only keeps ourselves hostage to sin. Thanks to God, we don't have to stay there in bondage, God says come home.

My friends, let me tell how good our God is. You see, my mom and I growing up, and part of my adulthood, we didn't see eye to eye. Ever since my dear little Daddy went to be with Jesus, Mom and I fell apart even more. There were times we didn't speak to one another; it was really heartbreaking, to say the least. That's when we really needed one another the most. Now we are closer than ever, I truly am thankful to have her as my mom. I couldn't imagine my life without her; she's become my friend in life as well as my mom.

Today, my friends, I want to thank my God in heaven most importantly, for the restoration of mine and my mom's relationship. Not only are we talking and getting along, we are also in such a better place now. Before, we argued and upset one another most of the time. Now thanks to God our Father in heaven, we have grown to love one another like God would have us to. With the help of God, we've grown closer to one another. God has given me such a love for her I know it's from Him. She has a heart of gold; she would do anything for anyone. She definitely would give her shirt off her back for someone in need. She loves much and makes sure she tells everyone about our Lord and Savior.

# 2

## Forgiveness: Your Past Does Not Define You

What is forgiveness? Unselfish love is the basis of true forgiveness. First Corinthians13:4–5 tells us, "Love is patient and kind, not jealous, not boastful, not proud, rude or selfish not easily angered, and it keeps no record of wrongs." Who are we if we don't forgive others their trespasses against us and expect God to forgive us of our trespasses? To answer this question, let's look at what God's word says.

Just as God is a gracious and merciful Father, we too should show grace and mercy to others. In Ephesians 4:32 we are commanded to, "Be kind to one another, tenderhearted, forgiving one another, even as God in Christ forgave you." Matthew 6:14 tells us, "For if you forgive men their trespasses, your Heavenly Father will also forgive you." Colossians 3:13 also says, "Bear with each other and forgive one another if any of you has a grievance against someone, forgive as the Lord forgave you." Finally, in 1 John 1:9, we are told that, "If we confess our sins, He is faithful and just to forgive us our sins, and cleanse us from all unrighteousness."

So if God is faithful and just to forgive us of all our sins, why are you running from Father God? Don't you want to be free from Satan's grip on your life? Just as Adam and Eve tried to hide in the garden after they sinned, sometimes we find ourselves trying to hide from God in this world.

Yes, everyone has done something, they're not proud of at one point or another. You may even feel that you are too bad of a person for God to forgive. You don't have to stay in your life of sinfulness. If He can pull me out of the pits of hell, He can do the same for you too.

Friends, let me tell you something. God is right there with you, everywhere you go. No matter where you are, in a dark alley or on a dark road, He's right there with you. There's no sin too great that God won't forgive you. All we have to do is realize that our lives aren't our own, and we belong to God. He's the one who gave us this life, and He's the one who can give us the free gift of eternal life. All we have to do is ask Him.

You're not defined by your past; that isn't who God says you are. God says you're His; you're beautifully made in His image, you're not a mistake, and you have a purpose and calling on your life. Second Corinthians 5:17 says, "Therefore if any man be in Christ, he is new creature, old things are passed away behold all things become new."

We all have issues we deal with on a daily basis. Remember this: You are wonderfully and beautifully made; God makes no mistakes. We may all look different on the outside, but we're all made the same on the inside. Don't let the world or Satan tell you you're not. Satan is a liar, and he wants to keep you bogged down with worry and self-pity. Satan wants to steal your joy, and one way that he tries to steal your joy is to bring up your past to you.

What happened yesterday is gone; today is a new beginning. You can't go back and change the past, but you can change your future. Live every day as if you're living for God. Live today like it's your last; tomorrow isn't promised to any of us. Live your best life today and enjoy the small things in life. Jeremiah 29:11 says, "For I know the thoughts that I think toward you, says the Lord thoughts of peace, and not of evil, to give you an expected end."

Sure, there were times in my life I wanted a do-over, but we can't do do-overs. We must move forward every day and forgive those who hurt us. We must love much and laugh a little harder.

We only have one chance in this world to live our lives; once we go to sleep in Christ, we can't say "I'm sorry." Be encouraged, my friends. You're not who you were yesterday, a week ago, or even a year ago. You are a masterpiece who our Father in heaven has personally made.

Take that chance, fall in love, and if that one doesn't work out, pick yourself up, and kick the dust off your shoes. Life is going to have its mishaps and disappointments, but keep going and hold your head up high. Don't let the world tell you can't because God says, "You can because I am, the I Am."

# 3

## You're Not a Mistake

You're not a mistake, and you're not that identification. You might've been an alcoholic, an addict, and maybe a prostitute. Yes, you were doing worldly things, but Christ has made you anew. You are a new creation in Him. You are no longer a victim of the world; you are a victor. You are victorious! You're more than a conqueror, you're an overcomer!

This is what I want you to do, put your hand over your heart. Feel that? That's called life. God didn't make a mistake by giving you your life. He chose to form your body and breathe life into you. He gave you a purpose in life; there's no mistakes in God's creation.

Look at yourself in the mirror and repeat after me. "I'm made in His image. I'm beautiful. I'm wanted. I have a purpose. I'm not a mistake. I have worth in Father God. I'm a child of the King. He loves me." You've been chosen as one of His masterpieces. God cherishes you; He cares for you, and you are His. God doesn't make junk. We don't have to hide under the shadows of the world. We don't need makeup to cover up God's creation. God doesn't see a face full of makeup. He sees you from the inside, who you really are. We don't have to put on a front for God. He knows exactly who we are, what we look like; with no filters or disguises, He knows exactly how many hairs are on our heads. He just wants us as we are.

We may think that we have to put on a front for the world, so we won't be judged. Are we afraid if someone actually saw the real us, they wouldn't like what they saw? You see, my friends, God sees all no matter what we are covering up, so why are we hiding? Are we hiding just like Adam and Eve were when God came looking for them after they had sinned? They were hiding because they realized they were naked and had sinned. God already knew they had disobeyed Him and had eaten from the tree. He also knew where they were, and He also knows where we are when we hide. He sees and knows all. Why would we want to hide from the one that sent His Son to die for us, the one that loves us unconditionally? No matter the mess ups and our setbacks, God still loves us. God doesn't expect us to be perfect; He knows our hearts, and we fail Him every day. That's where grace and mercy come in, also forgiveness and salvation.

# 4

## Entering in Covenant with God

My dear friends, what does entering in covenant with God mean to you? Does it mean that you're making a promise, or is it deeper than that? To me, it is a sacred vow that is more binding than any legal, worldly document. Is it something you take very seriously? Do you hold it close to your heart?

In April 2021, God led me to enter into a marriage covenant with Him and Him alone. I don't mean a marriage covenant that is earthly, like that between a husband and wife. I'm talking about a heavenly covenant between you and Father God. A covenant more loving and intimate, no, it's not a sexual covenant; its beyond our finite minds in description.

Over the next month, I started talking with my pastors and their wives about what God had placed on my heart. They were all in agreement, and they felt the Holy Spirit was truly leading me into this covenant with God. A love covenant between Father God and you, it's a special moment, giving your life to Him. Surrendering your everything letting God, be your pilot and you take the co-pilot seat.

God put on my heart to write vows for Him, in that I was giving everything to Him. My life, my children, and if it be His will, my future earthly husband. After much prayer and seeking guidance from the Holy Spirt, my vows were complete.

I wanted to be obedient in everything I was doing, and I wanted people to see God most importantly. Satan tried to discourage me from entering into this covenant; he even persuaded some of my family and friends to be against it. I started getting discouraged and thinking to myself, "I'm not doing this." Truth be told, I almost threw in the towel.

Some people thought I was being just silly and making things up just to bring attention to myself. Some people told me to just go in front of the church and say that I'm in covenant with God. What they didn't understand was this. It went so much deeper than just feelings; I was feeling led by God. I was not going to be ashamed or embarrassed about the conviction He had placed on my heart. It wasn't coming from Deanna; it was God having me to walk out in obedience.

The day came, June 5, 2021, it was a beautiful Sabbath day. We had a wonderful worship service at church that morning, and there was just a certain beauty about the whole day. Leading up to the evening, my heart was overflowing with joy. What a wonderful Sabbath to have this beautiful, covenant ceremony, as the following day was (Shavuot) Pentecost.

As I stood in my living room with my two children by my side, my pastors and their families, and some really close friends, the covenant ceremony began. My pastors read scriptures; we prayed together, and I read my vows to Father God "Yahweh." The song I give myself away was playing, it was really beautiful. I would like to share with you my vows if I could.

> I give myself to You, my Husband. this is my public confession to be faithful, pure, and clean. I'm no longer tainted or dirty; you have washed me clean. I'm no longer the woman I was. You have changed me and cleansed me; You made me a better woman; I am forgiven and made brand-new. I am Your bride. You are my heart's desires, and my Husband. I want to give You all my whole heart, my body, my life; I am Yours. You

are my everything: my first love, my best friend. Without *You*, I'm nothing. I thank you, my King, for all you have brought me through. From this day forward, I give my love to You. I give my home, my children, my life, and my devotion to you. All that I have is yours; all that I am is yours. Yeshua, I love You more than anything. You have blessed me beyond all measure. Yeshua, my Husband, I thank You in advance for blessing me with a godly man and an earthly Husband. I ask that He loves You and puts You first above all things. I ask that He accepts me as I am and loves my children as his own. I promise to keep You dear to my heart and love You unconditionally. You are the head of my heart and my life. All that I do, let it be of You.

Through obedience and going through with the ceremony, Yahweh really blessed me. If it weren't for Him and my church family, I couldn't had done it. I'm one that can't get up in front of anyone, without being nervous as a cat. Father God gave me the courage to stand in front of my family and friends to give my whole life to Him. It was and is the most beautiful experience with Father God. It was one of the best days of my life, being able to commit myself fully to God.

Yes, I was ridiculed afterward by some people, but that's okay. I had done what God had wanted me to do. All my life I was just going through the motions, I didn't do what God would have me to do. I never showed Christ or even told others about Him. My prayer is that God's presence is strongly felt when others are around me. I want my life reflecting Him in every way. I didn't start well; I just really want to finish well in my Lord and Savior.

## Love Conquers All

Over the next month, a group of my sisters, and I from our congregation started dancing in the parks for our Lord. We just really wanted to show Christ to others through dance. One of my dearest friends said to me one day, "How would you feel about being set up with someone?" I said, "Okay." Now let me explain something to you. I'm one of these girls that don't do blind dates, but I was willing to give it a try.

Throughout the summer, we would meet up at different parks on Tuesdays to dance. On this particular day, we met up; my friend Nicole tells us there's a man coming to join us, and he was going to play his flute for us. Needless to say, I didn't expect to meet my future husband that evening. Let me tell you something, honey, when God does something, He goes big.

There we were, dancing and praising God and up walks a really handsome man. I remember thinking, *Wow, he's really good looking.* Little did I know, God had orchestrated this meeting all along. I remember how nice and polite he was, and he was nicely dressed, as if he was going to church. He came right over and stood right next to me. Before we started to dance, we gathered into a circle to pray. Without hesitating, he reached down and held my hand; I remember thinking, *Wow, what a gentleman.* After praying, we started to dance and getting acquainted as we went along. After some time, we sat down to rest. As we sat there talking, he pulled out his flute and started to play. It was so beautiful.

Later that evening, I remembered getting home and looking him up on Facebook. I had to know all about him "in a stalker kind of way." We both looked one another up trying to find out more about one another. Finally, we found each other and started talking, and we talked and talked for hours that night. Leading up to our first date he picks me up from my house with a rose in his hand. He even asked to meet my mom; he wanted to ask her for permission to take me out on a date. To my mom's surprise, she had never been asked by anyone if they could take her daughter out before. That really touched my heart getting my mom's blessing. As we went on our first date, we just really started laying everything out on the table. We set for hours, just talking and crying, just being up front with one another. We both had a past that we weren't proud of, but with God, we were able to give each other our testimonies with no judgment. He wiped my tears away, as we talked getting to know one another. We started our journey dating becoming inseparable. If we weren't calling, we were going to see each other each day.

After dating for a month, David asked me to marry him. David and I dated five months, and we were married on December 3, 2021. I truly married my best friend. He was, and is, what I prayed for. I couldn't ask God for better because I've married the best.

Have you ever met someone you instantly connected with? That's exactly what happened, and we felt like we had known one another for years. God sent us to each other; He knew exactly we needed each other. He definitely answered my prayers. David was exactly who I prayed for and more. He's a true man of God; he has a love for God's people, especially the lost, it really warms my heart. By his example, talking to others about Christ unashamed, truly God's love radiates through him.

Thanks to our really good friend, and most importantly God, we have a great life together. Isn't it funny how God works? God takes something or someone broken and makes them whole again. He took two broken families and blended our families together, and now the seven of us are complete. You say seven, but wait, there's only six. Yes, seven is correct. There's God as our cornerstone, David, me and our four children, so that makes the seven of us. We didn't know what we were missing from our lives until God brought us together. My heart is overjoyed having the seven of us together. I thank my Father in heaven for our life and family.

# 5

## *My Heart's Desire*

My heart's desire is to know Him so much more. To bring others to Christ, furthering God's kingdom. My life is far from perfect, but with God by my side and working through me, I'm a much better woman. I feel that my life has paralleled the life of Mary Magdalene in that we both struggled with problems and strayed from God. We are both repentant sinners and became followers of Christ. I was a very sinful woman; now I am redeemed, and I'm no longer a slave to sin.

No, our marriage isn't perfect, but with God (Yahweh), our life is good. We are very happy; yes, life has its issues, but with God, we have weathered the storm. Today yes, we still have our day-to-day struggles, but with God as our cornerstone, we are stronger. Life throws us curveballs along the way, but we are holding tight to our Father in heaven. We are a work in progress, I thank my God above; I'm not where I used to be, or the person I was. I'm a daughter of the most-high God, and I've been set free. I want to thank God that I have a godly man that leads our home with no apologies. He's everything I've prayed for and so much more. Before bed, we read God's word and pray every day. I pray this encourages you as you read this book.

In Ephesians 1:7–8, "In Him we have redemption through His blood, the forgiveness of sins according to the riches of His grace which He made to abound toward us in all wisdom and prudence. Our sins and transgressions were covered by the blood of Christ through His sacrifice, dying for all of us." He took the beatings, shed His blood; that is what you call love. Joshua 24:15 tells us, "As for me and my house we will serve the Lord."

# 6

## Who Is the I Am?

John 6:35 states, "I am the bread of life, he who comes to me, shall never hunger, and he who believes in Me shall never thirst."

John 6:51, 53, 54 states,

> I am the living bread which came down from Heaven, if any man eat of this bread he shall live forever, and the bread that I will give is My flesh which I will give for the life of the world.... Then Jesus said unto them, Verily, Verily I say unto you, except you eat the flesh of the Son of Man, and drink His blood, ye have no life in you.... Whosoever eats My flesh and drinks My blood, hath eternal life, and I will raise him up at the last day.

John 8:12 states, "Then Jesus spoke to them again, saying I am the light of the world, he who follows Me shall not walk in darkness, but have the light of life."

John 10:7, 9 states, "Then Jesus said to them again, most assuredly, I say to you, I am the door of the sheep,...I am the door, if anyone enters by Me, He will be saved and will go in and out and find pasture."

John 10:11 states, "I am the good shepherd: the good shepherd giveth His life for the sheep."

John 14:6 states, "Jesus said to him, I am the way, the truth, and the life, no man cometh unto the Father but by Me."

John 15:5 states, "I am the vine, you are the branches, he that abides in me, and I in him, the same bringeth forth much fruit, for without Me you can do nothing."

Through Him, we are saved, through Him we are forgiven, redeemed and forever changed. You don't have to go through life alone, He is always there, even in the silence. Get alone with God, that's all you need. Getting in your quite time with God, praying in the stillness of silence with Him. Find a closet, an empty room… just sit in His presence. Take a drive, turn the radio off, you can have a wonderful conversation with God just driving down the road. He speaks to us through our hearts and minds.

## Road to Salvation

For all have sinned and come short of the glory of God. Being justified freely by His grace through the redemption that is in Christ Jesus. Whom God hath set forth to be a propitiation through faith in His blood to declare His righteousness for the remission of sins that are passed through the forbearance of God. (Romans 3:23–25)

But God commanded His love toward us, in that while we were yet sinners, Christ died for us. (Romans 5:8)

For the wages of sin is death, but the gift of God is eternal life through Jesus Christ our Lord. (Romans 6:23)

But if we walk in the light, as He is in the light, we have fellowship, one with another and the blood of Jesus, His son cleanses us from all sins. If we say we have no sin, we deceive ourselves and the truth is not in us. If we confess our sins, He is faithful and just to forgive us our sins and to cleanse us from all unrighteousness. (1 John 1:7–9)

As far as the east is from the west, so far hath He removed our transgressions from us. Like as a father pitied his children, so the Lord pitied them that fear Him. For He knows our frame, He remembers that we are dust. As for man, his days are as grass: as a flower of the field, so He flourished. For the wind passed over it, and it is gone; and the place thereof shall know it no more. But the mercy of the Lord is from everlasting to everlasting upon them that fear Him, and His righteousness unto children's children. (Psalms 103:12–17)

Words of Encouragement

I can do all things through Christ which strengthened me. (Philippians 4:13)

Who comforted us in all our tribulation, that we may be able to comfort them which are in any trouble, by the comfort wherewith we ourselves are comforted of God. For as the sufferings of Christ abound in us, so our consolation also abounded by Christ. (2 Corinthians 1:4, 5)

Cast thy burden upon the LORD, and he shall sustain thee: he shall never suffer the righteous to be moved. (Psalm 55:22)

These things I have spoken unto you, that in me ye might have peace. In the world ye shall have tribulation: but be of good cheer; I have overcome the world. (John 16:33)

And in that day ye shall ask me nothing. Verily, verily, I say unto you, Whatsoever ye shall ask the Father in my name, he will give it you…. Hitherto have ye asked nothing in my name: ask, and ye shall receive, that your joy may be full. (John 16:23, 24)

Through Him we are saved, through Him we are forgiven, redeemed, and forever changed. You don't have to go through life alone. He is always there, even in the silence. Get alone with God, that's all you need. Getting in your quite time with God, praying in the stillness of silence with Him. Find a closet, an empty room… just sit in His presence. Take a drive, turn the radio off, you can have a wonderful conversation with God just driving down the road. He speaks to us through our hearts and minds.

# 7

## Who Are You to Christ?

Do you believe that you have been chosen? Your identity is one of a kind; it's like a special fingerprint not one is the same. Yeah, we may look alike in some ways or another, but that doesn't mean you're the same person. You are God's creation, He knew you before you were born, way before the earth even existed. He formed your little body in your mother's womb, seeing a beautiful masterpiece. When you were born yes, you were helpless and such a little thing. That doesn't mean God didn't already have plans for your life.

He knew the mistakes you would make in life, the messes that you would get into. He knew we would have a sinful nature and that we would stray. That's where He sent His Son, His one and only Son to take away all our sin debt. He took all the humiliation being mocked and persecuted, and He was naked being nailed to the cross.

Talking about humiliation in front of the whole world. You know what, though, He never once complained about anything at all. They whipped Him so bad, He wasn't recognizable when they were finished with Him. Not only did they whip Him; they also pulled out His beard. They put a crown of thorns in His head. They spit in his face; they slapped Him, and He still stood there and took it. Not only did they mock Him; they cast lots over *His clothing*. Can you imagine clothes taking the place of our Savior?

After hanging on the cross, He saw what they were doing and said, "Father, forgive them for they know not what they do." That's how much love He has for us. It takes a lot of courage and humility to do what *He did*. Could you stand there and take the whipping, the beating, the spitting in your face, the crown of thorns in your head, what about your beard ripped out? Could you take it like our Savior did?

Even now could you forgive others for what they did to you? Okay, let's go a little further; what about someone hurting your spouse, family, or your children? Would you allow that? Most wouldn't stand there and watch them being hurt; most would jump in the way before allowing that to take place.

With every pound of the nail being nailed, every stripe He received, every slap in the face, we were on His mind. Could you take the pain of being nailed to a cross and hanging there for hours before you die? Imagine stepping on a nail and that going through your foot, how painful that is. Now it sets up infection you have to go to the doctor to have medicine to help with the infection. Even worse, that it sets up as gain green you have to have an amputation. What then? Sure, you get through the surgery just fine and go on to live your life.

Now imagine a nail a hundred times bigger that went through Jesus's hands and feet. He didn't have medicine to take away the infection or pain. He could've called ten thousand angels to come take Him down, but He didn't. With every struggling breath we were on His mind, losing all that blood, being very dehydrated, barely able to function, disoriented, blinded with blood and sweat. But the most painful of it all, God turned His back on His son Jesus. But He didn't turn away from Jesus or leave Him he couldn't look upon the sin.

He had all the sins of the world on Him, sins that we have committed and going to commit. Could you imagine, gasping for air as you pushed up to get a breath; then with your whole body weight pulling you back down. With each breath you took it was even harder. You start to feel exhausted you can't go on. That's exactly how our Savor felt on that dreadful day hanging there for all mankind. That's how much love He has for you and me. Even for the ones He knew would reject Him and just imagine He did that for Hitler too. All those lives that were taken oh but wait, He still loved Him enough to die for him too. One would say he's a terrible person; he killed God's chosen people how could he be loved and forgiven?

Jesus didn't pick and choose a certain few who He was dying for. Jesus doesn't work that way; He died for all mankind. He was the perfect sacrifice that was spotless in every way.

Where would you be without Him? I certainly wouldn't be where I'm at if it weren't for Him. Most likely, I'd probably not be here. Let's go a little further where would you be today without Christ? What has he done for you?

I can tell you from experience my life has gotten so much better since I let God take the reins of my life. Yes, I still get sick; I still struggle every day just like everyone else does. Yes, I lose my way, lose sight of the Father, trying to do things on my own, but He reaches down pulls me right back up. I even need to have His correction at times, but I'm a work in progress.

No matter how much you have strayed, God is just a hand reach away. You may feel like you're too far to come back, but you're not. You may feel like you're not deserving of love and forgiveness, but yes you are. I can't tell you how many times God has brought me back. One would think after so many times they'd get tired of picking you back up. That's not the way God works. You see, His mercy and love go beyond skin deep.

You can't put God in a bottle nor in a box. He's much too big for that. My God is much bigger, and our problems aren't too much for Him to handle. We can go to our Father in heaven about anything. He's a big God; there's nothing He can't handle. He's not going to laugh at or judge you. People may laugh or judge you but that's okay. They just don't understand that everyone is made different. We're different for a reason; we're not supposed to be the same. If we were all the same, this world would be a boring place. We have different personalities and different thought processes. This world may leave you, but you know what God won't. He never left me when I messed up and hurt Him, for sure He won't leave you either in your darkest moments. God is faithful; He's the one that's going to stick by you no matter what.

His grace, mercy, forgiveness brings peace, joy, and happiness; and love conquers all. You don't ever want to take your eyes off God and, you end up off-roading. You find yourself up the creek without a paddle, so to speak. Always remember that your lifeguard walks on water. He calms the raging storms in our lives, and the wind that beats against the sails. He controls everything with his hands and His voice. With His words, he says, "Peace be still." Mark 4:39 tells us and He arose and rebuked the wind and said unto the seas, "Peace be still" and the wind ceased and there was a great calm.

He can calm our nerves, our hearts, and our minds. Don't focus on your weaknesses; focus on His strength. Be strong and be of good cheer. Isaiah 41:10 also says, "So do not fear, for I am with you; do not be dismayed, for I am your God. I will strengthen you and help you. I will uphold you with my righteous right hand." Isaiah 46:10 also says, "He says 'be still and know that I AM God. I will be exalted among the nations; I will be exalted in the earth.'" Philippian's 4:13 also says, "I can do all things through Christ who gives me strength."

# 8

## Loving Your Neighbors as Yourself Being the Light for Others

The Bible talks about loving your neighbor as yourself. Matthew 22:37–39 tells us, "Thou shalt love the lord thy God with all thine heart, and with all thine soul, and all thy mind. This is the first and great commandment; and the second is like unto the it thou shalt love thy neighbor as thyself."

Do we actually love our neighbors as ourselves? Or are we simply hiding behind a mask? Are we being a beacon in the night? Are we allowing God to shine through us for everyone to see? Matthew 5:15–16 tells us, "Neither do men light a candle, and put it under a bushel, but on a candlestick; it gives light unto all that are in the house. Let your light so shine before men that they may see your good works, and glorify your Father which is in Heaven."

We need to let God's light shine everywhere we are. John 8:12 tells us, "Again Jesus spoke to them, saying "I am the light of the world. Whoever follows me will not walk in darkness, but will have the light of life."

Be the light to others so when theirs goes out, there's still light. How can we be the beacon in the night? Love on that person who is hurting, be the one who stands out from the crowd, who goes the extra mile to extend a helping hand. Jesus tells us that whatever you do for the least of these, you do for me. A small amount of darkness cannot make a difference in a lit room, but a little light in a dark room can disperse a great amount of darkness.

# 9

## Where Would You Be Without Jesus?

You're going through life just thinking, "Hey, I've got this, I don't need anyone…No one is going to tell me what to do…I can do whatever I want." Then it happens. You get caught shoplifting, but you think you don't have to abide by the law. You think, "I'm my own boss. I'll get out of this." Yes, you go to jail and spend a week there. One of your family members bails you out, so what are you going to do now? Are you going to get your life back on track, or do you slip back into your old ways? Will you find yourself homeless and out on the streets? How many times does it take for us to tell ourselves, "Enough is enough"?

After some point, when you're cold and hungry, you start to realize you were once on top of the world; you had a good job, a house to live in, you were going somewhere, but now you're down to nothing. Your entire life has spiraled out of control. You realize in that moment; you have got to do something about it. Now imagine, a man walks up and says, "I'll take your place," and that man is Jesus. He wants to take away our sorrows, our filthiness, and our transgressions.

After Jesus agrees to take your place, do you allow Him to take your place or do you tell Him, "No, thank you, I can handle this on my own." He's already paid the debt we owed; all we have to do is accept Him into our hearts. Today, Jesus is knocking. Are we willing to accept Him today? Is it possible that we might think we don't need a Savior? Do we think our sins aren't that bad, and we don't need saving. We might even think to ourselves, "My sins aren't as bad as others, I do a lot of good deeds. Aren't my good deeds outweighing my bad? Jesus will see how my good deeds outweigh my bad; I just know He'll let me slide by…"

Can you imagine if Jesus didn't go to the cross? What then… how would we be saved? Without His salvation, His work on the cross would be void. We as humans can't atone for our own transgressions and sins; you see, salvation doesn't work that way. Jesus doesn't force Himself on you to believe in Him or come to salvation. He would love to have you come to Him; it's a heart choice and a change. We need to want to come to Him; He won't make you do anything you're not ready for. He waits patiently; He doesn't wait until it's our timing, only His timing. The enemy will try to keep you from accepting Christ as your Savior.

He will try to say, "You're defeated…there's nothing for you… you're not good enough and worthless." God says, "*No*, you aren't defeated and worthless. *Yes*, there is something for you, and you are good enough." Each one of us are made in His own image, and we're uniquely made. It doesn't matter how the world or Satan views us; it only matters how God views us. Satan knows his days are numbered, and there's nothing he can do about it. He'll try to do all he can to take as many people with him into the fiery pit. Imagine how precious your soul is in that both God and Satan want it.

God loves us so much that He's a sovereign and just Father. He doesn't keep score on how much we've had to be picked back up. He doesn't condemn you and throw you away. He doesn't leave us stranded, nor high and dry. He says do you trust me to carry you through?

Keep holding on to the Father, never letting go of His hand. Time and time again, we let go of the Father's hand losing our way, but God keeps bringing us back with wide open arms. He says come home, my child. That's something about our God; He doesn't let you go. You hear the words "You're in a rut" and start doubting yourself; that's Satan telling you another lie.

With Jesus, there's always a way. He's a way maker, a promise-keeper. He says, "Come as you are, all who are weary and heavy laden, I will give you rest." Most certainly, we all get down and discouraged from time to time, but Jesus is our redeemer.

Do you have a personal relationship with Jesus? Do you want to know Him today? You don't have to have an elaborate prayer; a simple and honest prayer that comes from the heart and brings true repentance. No, you don't have to repeat after anyone to come to Christ. All you need to do is ask Him to forgive you of your sins and turn from your ways. Ask Him to come into your heart and save you. We all need a savior to take away our sins. Are you willing to let Him today?

Let Him change you completely. Let go and let God. He's waiting patiently on us to fully reach out and call upon His mighty precious name. By giving Jesus your heart and life, your life will be forever changed. Jesus won't force you, He's a gentleman waiting for you to accept Him as your Savior.

# 10

## Are You Putting on the Full Armor of God?

We must put on the full armor of God. Ephesians 6:13–17 tells us,

> Wherefore take unto you the whole armor of God, that ye may be able to withstand in the evil day, and having done all, to stand. Stand therefore, having your loins girt about with truth, and having on the breastplate of righteousness; and your feet the shod with preparation of the gospel of peace; above all, taking the shield of faith, wherewith ye shall be able to quench all the fiery darts of the wicked. And take the helmet of salvation, and the sword of the Spirit, which is the Word of God.

Are you on the defending side of Christ, or are you hiding? What does it look like defending our Lord and Savior? Knowing Jesus died freely for us, would you defend Him? What does a soldier for Christ look like? Anyone who puts on the full armor of God, who is willing to fight for our King and lay down their lives for Him and surrender everything for Him…that's a soldier for Christ.

Do we truly leave all our possessions behind and follow Christ? So what does that mean to you? To me, my friends, that means giving up everything and trusting that Jesus will make a way and provide for us. We as humans have great possessions that most wouldn't let go of. Not one of us could say that we've left everything behind for the sake of Jesus Christ. Are we putting our possessions before our Lord Jesus? My friends, we all have put something in front of Jesus, our family, our homes, finances, our jobs etc. Every one of us have been guilty of putting our personal things ahead of Jesus. Imagine if we all sold all that we had and left everything behind and followed Christ.

Matthew 19:21 tells us, "Jesus said unto him, 'If thou wilt be perfect, go and sell what thou hast and give to the poor, and thou shalt have treasure in Heaven, and come and follow me.'"

There's nothing like having that relationship with Him. With *Christ* in your life and letting Him be the head of your home, and He can change your life for the better. He's our cornerstone of our lives, and we owe everything to Him. Just like you and your spouse having that love for one another, you must have God as your cornerstone in your marriage. The closer the both of you get to God, the closer you get to one another. You see, it's a love triangle and each point keep leading up to God.

Would you rather stand with God and be judged by the world or stand with the world being judged by *God*? At judgment day, every knee will bow every soul will confess that Jesus is King of kings and Lord of lords. Do you want to hear our Lord say, "Well done, thy good faithful servant, thou have been faithful over many things enter now for great is your reward"? Or would you rather hear, "Depart from me I never knew you, *you workers of iniquity*"?

# 11

## Praising Him in the Waiting

What does "praise Him in the waiting" look like? Maybe you've been praying for healing for many years, you begin to think, is God hearing my prayers? My friend, He hears all our prayers. Sometimes while waiting for answers, what are we doing about it? I'm sure all of us get impatient, waiting and waiting; but you know, even though we think God isn't listening, or we feel He's a million miles away, He's never left us not once. He tells us He will never leave us nor forsake us.

Many times do we try to get ahead of God in a job or a relationship that we are so desperately trying to get? Do we put (Yahweh) God in a bubble or in a box? We think we have to limit Him, but you see, He doesn't work that way. He works on His schedule, and His timing, not ours. He's not a "sometimes Father"; He's an "all-the-time Father." At times, He's wanting us to be still and silent and just listen to Him. In the silence, you can hear more clearly what He is wanting to say.

In the trials and tribulations, we yearn to hear His voice. We want Him to speak to us, and those are times He really wants to do a mighty work in us. Psalms 46:10 says, "Be still and know that I Am God." John 14:1 tells us, "Let not your heart be troubled, you believe in God believe also in Me."

Have you ever thought about why some people with illnesses are completely healed and some aren't? The healing on earth is temporary, but eternal healing is forever. It's not a lack of faith of a person that determines their healing; however, God has a reason as to why they remain sick and not receive healing right away. He has a purpose for our lives, though we may not see it right away; it may look or feel your healing may not come. Rest assured either healing comes here on earth or heavenly healing after we rest in Him.

Many times, in life, we think is this ever going to pass from me? At times, we think is God hearing our prayers, and other times, we might say to ourselves, "God, where are you?" He's always listening to us as we pray; just maybe He has other things in store down the road.

We are to praise Him either way; I know it's hard to see the big picture in front of us. What if God decides to take you home for you to receive your heavenly healing? Your heavenly healing is eternal; healing here on earth is only temporary. Maybe you're in remission from cancer, and one day you start feeling sick again and you don't understand what's going on; you start asking God why? You think to yourself, "Are my prayers not enough?" "I seek Him, I'm faithful in reading His word, and I share Jesus with others. Is God not listening?" My friends, maybe the greater healing is after He calls you home. Yes, the ones that you leave behind are hurting, but joy comes in the morning.

You might find yourself sitting in a waiting room, worried about a loved one, not knowing the answers as to what's going on? Are we trusting God and praising Him during this trying time, no matter the outcome? God heals on His timing; the healing may be down the road a way. We must never cease to pray; God is listening to our prayers. Praise Him in the waiting, in the unknown, the unsure times of desperation; seek Him diligently. Yes, life is hard, but God is still on the throne, in the good and bad times. God has a greater purpose, even when we can't see it. He's working behind the scenes on our behalf.

I want you to do something. Close your eyes and take a big deep breath and exhale. Didn't that feel good, to take a good deep breath? Now, remember who gave you that breath. God is the one that breathed the breath of life into our bodies. Without His breath in us, we as humans wouldn't make it one second.

At the beginning of the world, when He spoke life into existence, God chose to give us life. He knew how we would be—a selfish generation in need of a savior. Without His saving grace, we would perish in the lake of fire. I thank God for His Son Jesus, for His life and testimony He left behind here on earth. He is and truly was the perfect one who lived and died for us. He's coming again to receive His people up and take us home with Him. Dearest brothers and sisters, are you ready to see him? Is your house in order to be called up in Him? Friends, if you're unsure, it's not too late to come to know Jesus as your personal savior.

He says come, no matter what you look like. You may be looking like a train wreck on the outside, but all that matters is what's in your heart. God doesn't look on the outer appearance, He's looking on the inside. All you need to do is call out to Him ask Him to save you, truly repent and turn from our evil ways. You will be saved and changed in that moment.

What does our hearts say about us? Proverbs 27:19–20 tells us, "As water reflects the face, so one's life reflects the heart. Death and destruction are never satisfied, and neither are human eyes." My husband has really shown me that Christ not only loves the church, but His love goes beyond. It's not just skin deep. He's taught me to look into someone's eyes and know Jesus died for them too. No matter the circumstances, it doesn't matter what you've done over your lifetime; you're still wanted and loved. God's love goes beyond skin deep; He looks at the person's heart.

Yes, you may have riches beyond what you can imagine, but if you don't have Jesus, you're spiritually broken. You can have all the riches, fans, fame, and fortune; but life without Jesus is only sadness. With Him, your life will be filled with joy, peace, and happiness. Yes, you can have joy, peace, and happiness without Jesus, but that's only temporary. With Him, it's everlasting. Do you want everlasting or temporary?

You may face problems and heartache, but joy comes in the morning; we must count it all joy. The hurting does stop, the anger we have does go away; we don't have to stay frustrated or bitter, we can choose to be happy. That's why we have a Savior who wipes away our tears and takes our hurt away.

This is how we fight our battles, getting down on our knees and fully giving it to God. It may look like you're surrounded by chaos, turmoil, and all the problems of the world; but we are surrounded by His presence, His Holy Spirit, His peace that calms our hearts. He's in the midst of the storms, in the valleys we walk through. He is with us now, no matter where we are, high or low in life. The Bible says over and over again, "Do not fear." Fear is a liar; do not be dismayed or let not your heart be troubled. Second Timothy 1:7 tells us, "For God gave us a spirit not of fear but of power and love self-control." First John 4:18 also says, "There is no fear in love, but perfect love casts out fear." Satan wants us to have fear, he doesn't want us to trust in our Lord and Savior."

That's so far from what God is telling us. God does love you; you are loved. He takes all the fear and doubt away. Are you willing to trust Him today? Let Him take the reins of life; step back and breathe. Take the backseat let God take the driver's seat.

He gently holds us in His arms, wiping our tears away. He gives us peace; takes away our pain and hurt; and renews our hearts, spirits, and minds. Joy comes in the morning; we may be fighting a battle, but the battle is already won. We may think to ourselves does it ever end? Yes, it does we must praise Him, keep our heads held high, knowing that our Father in heaven will bring us through. You see, we need our Father in heaven to grow in our walk with Him. God never promises us a life of luxury. We need Him in every moment of our lives. He came as a baby putting on a human suit the first time; the next time we see Him, He's coming back as King of kings and Lord of lords.

# 12

## Soldier for Christ

Have you ever thought about where you would be without Jesus?

You're going through life just thinking, *Hey, I've got this, I don't need anyone…No one is going to tell me what to do…I can do whatever I want.* Then it happens. You get caught shoplifting, but you think you don't have to abide by the law. You think, *I'm my own boss, I'll get out of this.* Yes, you go to jail and spend a week there. One of your family members bails you out, so what are you going to do now? Are you going to get your life back on track, or do you slip back into your old ways? Well, you find yourself homeless and out on the streets? How many times does it take for us to tell ourselves, "Enough is enough?"

After some point, you're cold and hungry; you start to realize you were once on top of the world. You had a good job, a house to live in, you were going somewhere, but now you're down to nothing. Your entire life has spiraled out of control. You realize in that moment you have got to do something about it. Now imagine, a man walks up and says, I'll take your place, and that man is Jesus. He wants to take away our sorrows, our filthiness, and our transgressions.

You see, my friends, that's exactly what Jesus did on that dark, dreadful day on the cross. He took the sins of the whole world upon Himself and paid for our salvation. Jesus didn't have to pay for our debts. He chose to, and He freely laid down His life for all mankind.

Can you think of anyone who would take your place? Someone who would take all the guilt and shame away for you? There is no one else who can. Only Jesus can take away all our sins and cleanse us from all our transgressions. After Jesus agrees to take your place, do you allow Him to take your place or do you tell Him, "No thank you, I can handle this on my own." He's already paid the debt we owed; all we have to do is accept Him into our hearts.

Today, Jesus is knocking. Are we willing to accept Him today? Is it possible that we might think we don't need a Savior? Do we think our sins aren't that bad, and we don't need saving. We might even think to ourselves, "My sins aren't as bad as others. I do a lot of good deeds. Aren't my good deeds outweighing my bad? Jesus will see how my good deeds outweigh my bad. I just know He'll let me slide by."

Can you imagine if Jesus didn't go to the cross? What then? How would we be saved? Without His salvation, His work on the cross would be void. We as humans can't atone for our own transgressions and sins; you see, salvation doesn't work that way.

Christ truly was selfless, loving, and compassionate toward others. His love radiated all around for all to see. He wasn't ashamed to show His Father's love. He walked among the people not worrying about what others thought of Him. Yes, they mocked and ridiculed him, but that didn't stop him from bringing the good news to the world. He's the beginning and the end, the Alpha and Omega. We didn't choose Him; He chose us, and He calls us friends.

You see, Jesus is the way, the truth, and the life. John 14:6: tells us, "Jesus told him I am the way, the truth and the life. No one comes to the Father except through me."

Satan will try to say, "You're defeated…there's nothing for you. You're not good enough and worthless."

God says, "*No*, you aren't defeated and worthless. *Yes*, there is something for you, and you are good enough."

Each one of us are made in His own image, and we're uniquely made. It doesn't matter how the world or Satan views us; it only matters how God views us. Satan knows his days are numbered. and there's nothing he can do about it. He'll try to do all he can to take as many people with him into the fiery pit. Imagine how precious your soul is in that both God and Satan want it.

God loves us so much that He's a sovereign and just Father. He doesn't keep score on how much we've had to be picked back up. He doesn't condemn you and throw you away. He doesn't leave us stranded, nor high and dry. He says do you trust me to carry you through? Keep holding on to the Father, never letting go of His hand. Time and time again, we let go of the Father's hand losing our way, but God keeps bringing us back, with wide open arms. He says come home my child. That's something about our God, He doesn't let you go. You hear the words "You can't" and start doubting yourself; that's Satan telling you another lie.

With Jesus, there's always a way. He's a waymaker, a promise keeper. He says, "Come as you are, all who are weary and heavy laden, I will give you rest." Most certainly, we all get down and discouraged from time to time, but Jesus is our redeemer. Do you have a personal relationship with Jesus? Do you want to know Him today? You don't have to have an elaborate prayer, a simple and honest prayer that comes from the heart and brings true repentance. No, you don't have to repeat after anyone to come to Christ. All you need to do is ask Him to forgive you of your sins and turn from your ways. Ask Him to come into your heart and save you. We all need a savior to take away our sins. Are you willing to let Him today?

Let Him change you completely. Let go and let God. He's waiting patiently on us to fully reach out and call upon His mighty precious name. By giving Jesus your heart and life, your life will be forever changed. Jesus won't force you, He's a gentleman waiting for you to accept Him as your Savior.

*Be still and know that I am God!*

Deanna loves her Lord and Savior more than anything. Throughout her life, she went to church and was taught about God. She loves sharing God with others, every chance she gets. She has a heart for the homeless and the hurting.

Deanna works as a CNA for a local hospital, and she is now married to her best friend. Together, they have four children between them: Anna, Andrew, Hannah, and Jesse. Deanna and her family are members of Borderview Christian Church in Elizabethton, Tennessee, and they are actively serving on the praise team where Deanna gets to sing for her Lord and Savior, and David plays the drums.

If it wasn't for our Lord and Savior, Deanna wouldn't be here today. Deanna prays that this book will inspire everyone to know their worth to God.